P is for Putt

A Golf Alphabet

Written by Brad Herzog and Illustrated by Bruce Langton

Photo reference for the Vare Trophy on the V page courtesy of the LPGA.
Photo reference for the Vardon Trophy on the V page courtesy of PGA of America.

Sleeping Bear Press

310 North Main Street, Suite 300
Chelsea, MI 48118
www.sleepingbearpress.com

THOMSON
✦
GALE ™

© 2005 Thomson Gale, a part of the Thomson Corporation.

Thomson, Star Logo and Sleeping Bear Press are trademarks
and Gale is a registered trademark used herein under license.

Printed and bound in Canada.

10 9 8 7 6 5 4 3 2 1

Library of Congress Cataloging-in-Publication Data

Herzog, Brad.
P is for putt : a golf alphabet / written by Brad Herzog ; illustrated by Bruce Langton.
p. cm.
Summary: "An A-Z pictorial for children including golf terms, rules, famous people,
and courses introduced with poems accompanied by expository text to provide
detailed information"—Provided by publisher.
ISBN 1-58536-252-2
1. Golf—Juvenile literature. 2. Alphabet books. I. Langton, Bruce, ill. II. Title.

GV968.H47 2005
796.352'35—dc22   2004027295

To my grandmother, Celia Roth Herzog,
who always made time for miniature golf.

BRAD

❖

To Rebecca—thanks for being by my side and being the
best mother for Brett and Rory, our blessings.

To all children who have decided to take up the sport of golf,
best of luck to all of you in the future.

My thanks to Sleeping Bear Press and
Brad Herzog for all their hard work.

BRUCE

A a

A is for the amateurs
who play golf everywhere,
from Alaska to Australia,
in weather foul or fair.

Golf is one of the few sports that can be played by people of all kinds—young and old, male and female, big and small. People love many things about the game, including the way it challenges you to keep improving, the enjoyment of spending a pleasant several hours in the outdoors, and the chance to roam the most beautiful playing fields in sports.

There are more than 16,000 golf courses in the United States alone, and over 25 million Americans play every year. Although professional golf is a popular spectator sport, most golfers are amateurs—people who are not paid for playing. In fact, golf is so much fun that people all around the world, from kids to senior citizens, are willing to pay to play the game. And they'll play anywhere! Every year, the frigid country of Greenland hosts the World Ice Golf Championship on an icy golf course surrounded by huge icebergs and visited by the occasional polar bear!

The par on a golf hole is determined by the distance between the tee and the green. If most good golfers can start on the tee and get the ball into a distant hole by hitting it five times (using five strokes), then par on that hole is 5. If you are able to get the ball in the hole in four strokes (one stroke under par), it is called a "birdie" because "bird" was a nineteenth-century term for anything excellent. A score of two strokes under par is called an eagle. A very rare three-under-par feat (such as a two on a par 5) is called a double eagle or an albatross. Bogey is the word for a one-over-par score. There are also double bogeys (two over par), triple bogeys (three over par), and quadruple bogeys (four over par). Most golf courses have a mixture of par 3 holes, par 4 holes, and par 5 holes.

B is for a birdie,
a very good golf score.
It's finishing a long par 5
with a score of four.

Many kids get a chance to learn about golf and improve their game by serving as caddies. A caddie may have several responsibilities. He or she may carry a player's golf bag, locate the player's golf ball along the course, keep the golf clubs clean, and even offer advice about club selection and course strategy.

Many golfers carry their own bags or place them on motorized golf carts. Golfers may include no more than 14 clubs in a bag. Each is designed to hit the ball a certain distance, and players are free to choose which 14 clubs are best suited to their game. There are two types of clubs—woods (longer, heavier clubs for longer shots) and irons (shorter clubs for shots requiring greater aim). Irons are made of steel. However, most woods are no longer made of wood, but rather a metal called titanium.

C also begins chip, a short, lofted shot usually taken from a spot near the green, and clubhouse, the main building at a golf course.

C is for the caddies
who carry clubs around.
They are golf's hardest workers
—at least, pound for pound.

A dimpled golf ball
delicately placed upon a tee.
A daring golfer drives it.
That's the letter D.

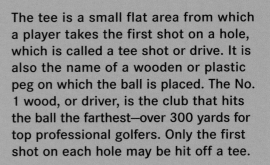

The tee is a small flat area from which a player takes the first shot on a hole, which is called a tee shot or drive. It is also the name of a wooden or plastic peg on which the ball is placed. The No. 1 wood, or driver, is the club that hits the ball the farthest—over 300 yards for top professional golfers. Only the first shot on each hole may be hit off a tee.

Early golfers played with a feather-filled leather ball. Modern golf balls are usually white, weighing 1.62 ounces and measuring 1.68 inches across. They may be wound (made of thin rubber thread wound around a core) or two-piece (made with no rubber thread). Both types are covered by a hard plastic shell containing hundreds of dimples, or tiny round dents, to help the ball fly farther.

D is also for divot, a piece of turf lifted out of the ground when a player swings.

E e

E is a round of eighteen holes,
nine holes on each side.
Some are long, some are short,
some narrow, and some wide.

In 1857 the Royal & Ancient Golf Club in St. Andrews, Scotland, which is often called the "Home of Golf," became the first course to consist of 18 holes. That has been the magic number ever since. Generally, 18-hole courses range from 6,000 to 7,000 yards long, but there are also nine-hole and shorter par-3 only courses, which are good beginner courses. Most 18-hole courses are laid out in two loops that bring the golfers back near the first tee after every nine holes. The first nine holes (front nine) are called going "out." The second nine holes (back nine) are coming "in." The halfway point (after nine holes) is called the "turn."

Each golf course and hole is unique. Some are built along the ocean or in the desert. Maybe the golfer must aim over a pond or between rows of tall trees. Many holes also include a "dogleg," which is a left or right bend in the fairway.

When you hit a shot that is going too far or wide and may be headed toward another golfer or a spectator, you are supposed to yell "Fore!" to alert them and protect them from getting hurt. The word is believed to come from either "forecaddie" (a person who stood where the ball might land to find it more easily) or "Beware before!" (a command that warned soldiers to drop to the ground).

F is also for fairway, the stretch of closely mowed grass that extends from the tee to the green. Golfers aim for the fairway because it is much easier to hit it well from there.

The flagstick, also often called the pin, is a movable pole placed in the hole to show its location on the green. The hole (which measures 4¼-inches across) is usually moved to a different spot each day. This is called the pin placement. The goal is to protect the greens (so that one area isn't constantly trampled) and to make golfers use different strategies for getting the ball close to the hole.

"Fore!" shouts the golfer
        to make sure folks are clear.
And F is for the flagstick,
    which should say, "Hey! Aim here!"

Ff

G g

Grab a glove and grip a club.
Golf with letter **G**.
Give a great big hand
to the grinning gallery.

The grip is the top part of a golf club, usually made from leather or rubber. It also means the way in which the club is held. The most common method of gripping a club is the Vardon, or overlapping grip, in which the pinky of the bottom hand overlaps between the index and middle fingers of the upper hand. To improve their grip, many golfers wear a golf glove, usually on their upper hand.

The gallery is another name for the spectators at a golf tournament. Usually they sit or stand behind ropes along the course. Unlike in most sports, golf fans are expected to keep quiet so that the golfers can concentrate.

G is also for Gene Sarazen and the greatest shot in golf history. In the final round of the 1935 Masters Tournament, Sarazen sank a shot from 225 yards away for a rare double eagle 2 on the par-5 15th hole. He went on to win the tournament.

A hole in one is scored when a golfer's first shot goes into the hole. Also called an ace, it is one of the hardest feats in sports. It is almost always accomplished on a par 3 hole, although some holes in one have occurred on holes more than 400 yards long! The youngest person ever to record an ace was just three years old (he did it on a short 65-yard hole). The oldest was 101!

H is also for handicap, a number that signifies a golfer's level of play based on recent scores. It adjusts a golfer's score, so that players of different ability may compete on equal terms. The best players are called "scratch" golfers and have a handicap of zero.

H also begins the last name of two golf legends. Walter Hagen won 11 major championships between 1914 and 1929 as the first great professional golfer. Ben Hogan won nine major championships between 1946 and 1953 and 61 PGA tournaments.

Hit the ball and watch it
disappear into the sun.
Holy cow! Hooray!
H is a hole in one!

Ii

I is for an iron shot
aimed toward an island green.
The goal? Just keep your golf ball
safe and dry and clean.

An island green is a green completely surrounded by water. It requires one of the more dramatic tee shots in golf, which is usually taken with an iron, a club with a thin bladelike head. Irons are numbered from 1 to 9. A 1-iron has only a slightly slanted clubface (the front of the clubhead). A 9-iron has a sharply slanted face. The greater the slant, the higher and shorter a ball will travel. A pitching wedge, which is even more slanted than a 9-iron, is used for short shots requiring the most accuracy. The more often a golfer plays, the better he or she becomes at judging exactly how far the ball will go with each iron.

I is also for Hale Irwin, who won three U.S. Open championships and then became the greatest player in the history of the Champions Tour. Formerly called the Senior Tour, the Champions Tour is for players who are age 50 or older.

It was April 1986 at the Masters Tournament. The "Golden Bear," 46-year-old Jack Nicklaus, had already won a record 17 major professional titles. But now some people were calling him the "Olden Bear" because he hadn't won a major in six years. Could he win again? Yes! With his son Jackie carrying his golf bag, Nicklaus played the final ten holes in seven strokes under par to come from behind and earn his sixth Masters and 18th major title. One last time, the "Golden Bear" had come out of hibernation!

The man who started the Masters Tournament (in 1934) was another **J**—legendary Bobby Jones. He was an attorney in Georgia who only rarely competed as an amateur golfer, but he still won 13 major tournaments in his brief career. In 1930 the 28-year-old Jones achieved golf's "Grand Slam" by winning the British Open, the British Amateur, the U.S. Open, and the U.S. Amateur. Seven weeks later he retired from competitive golf.

J is for Jack Nicklaus,
who was the very best.
In 18 major tournaments,
Jack outscored the rest.

Jj

K k

Arnold Palmer learned to play golf at the age of three, using a sawed-off set of clubs. He learned much about the game as a caddie and then won two Pennsylvania state high school golf titles and a U.S. Amateur championship. But it was his performance as a professional that led to his nickname—"The King." From 1958 to 1964, Palmer won seven major championships, and he did it with style and with smiles. He became so popular that huge crowds began to follow him on the golf course. The crowds became known as "Arnie's Army."

K is also for kids who love to play golf as much as their parents do. In fact, hundreds of kids from all over the world compete each year in the U.S. Kids Golf World Championship, a tournament for boys and girls ages 4 to 12. You're never too young to pick up a golf club and try out your swing. Just make sure the clubs are the right size! They shouldn't be any longer than the distance between your arms and the floor when you hold your arms straight out at your side.

K is for "the King."
Arnold Palmer is his name,
the most beloved golfer
ever to play the game.

The Ladies Professional Golf Association began in 1950 with nine tournaments and $50,000 in total prize money. Today LPGA players compete for more than $40 million in prize money. The four annual major LPGA tournaments are the Kraft Nabisco Championship, the LPGA Championship, the U.S. Women's Open, and the Women's British Open. Another **L** is Nancy Lopez, who won nine tournaments and Player of the Year honors in her first year on the LPGA Tour in 1978.

A links course is a golf course located along the seashore. The earliest courses in Scotland were links courses, and the British Open is always played on one.

L is also for lie. In golf, a lie means the ball's position on the ground. It can be a good lie (resting cleanly on the grass) or a bad lie (buried deep in the rough).

L is for the ladies
on the LPGA Tour
and all lovely links courses
built along the shore.

M is for the Masters,
  where the top pros try to hack it.
The winner of this magic major
  gets a cool green jacket.

The Masters Tournament is the only major PGA tournament always played on the same course. Each April it takes place at beautiful Augusta National Golf Club in Augusta, Georgia, which is famous for its magnolia trees (another M). In 2003 and 2004, two more M's—Mike Weir and Phil Mickelson—became the first two lefthanders to win the tournament's famous green jacket, which was originally designed to identify members of the golf club.

M is for miniature golf, too, a game featuring 18 miniature holes but only one club—the putter. Many mini golf courses have silly themes and trick holes, but some are serious challenges. There are even professional miniature golfers who compete in the Masters National Championship in Myrtle Beach, South Carolina.

M also begins mulligan, which is a chance to replay your last shot (if fellow players allow it) because you weren't happy with the result. Taking a mulligan isn't allowed in official tournaments.

N is for a number
　　written down on a scorecard.
　Add the holes up and you find...
　　　　　golf is pretty hard.

GOLF

	PAR								
520	400	130	354	445	418	220	518		
403	365	120	331	409	381	180	489		
394	275	80	224	313	288	129	388		
5	4	3	4	4	4	3	5	PAR	
6	4	3	5	5	4	3	5		
7	5	3	4	5	4	4	5		
	1	2	3	4	5	6	7	8	9

A golfer records the score for each hole on a scorecard. Golfers can compete against themselves by trying to achieve their lowest score, or they can compete against opponents in stroke play or match play. In stroke play, the golfer who finishes with the lowest total score is the winner. Most professional tournaments use stroke play for 72 holes (four 18-hole rounds). In match play, players or teams compete hole by hole. The player who needs the fewest number of strokes wins a hole. If there is a tie, the hole is said to be halved. Whoever wins the most holes takes the match.

N is also for the great Byron Nelson. In 1945 he won a remarkable 11 PGA tournaments in a row!

Another **N** is niblick, which was the name of a 9-iron before clubs were given numbers. Other early clubs had names like brassie, spoon, baffy, cleek, and mashie.

N
n

Oh my! Oh boy! **O** is for
the Open Championship.
Played in old Great Britain,
it's always worth the trip.

O o

Some historians trace golf back to a game called paganica, which was played by the Romans more than 1,600 years ago. But the first record of any mention of the word "golf" came from Edinburgh, Scotland, in 1457. That year King James II banned the sport because he wanted his subjects to practice archery instead. Edinburgh was also where the first known rules of the game were drawn up in 1744.

An open championship means that professionals and skilled amateurs may be invited to the tournament if they perform well in regional qualifying tournaments beforehand—maybe even in your hometown! Only one tournament is the Open Championship. Also known as the British Open, it is the oldest major tournament in golf. Eight men competed in the first tournament in 1860. Today, more than 100 of the world's top golfers travel to the British Isles in July to compete for the silver Claret Jug, which was first awarded way back in 1873.

The purpose of a putt is to roll the ball into the hole by using the only club that isn't slanted (the putter). This occurs on the putting green, which is the small area of extremely low-cut grass at the end of the fairway. The golfer whose ball is farthest from the hole putts first. Often, the rest of the players pick up their golf balls and mark their location with a coin or flat ball marker.

"Reading the green" means judging how hard the ball should be hit (the speed) and where you should aim. Where you aim is determined by the break, which is the direction the ball curves as it rolls toward the hole. This depends on which way the green slopes.

P is also for private courses (requiring membership to play) and public courses (open to everyone for a fee). Perhaps the most famous public course in the U.S. is another P—Pebble Beach in California.

Read the green. Judge the speed.
Aim it and… Guess what?
P is for a score of par.
You've made a perfect putt.

Q q

Q is found in Q School,
      where golfers qualify
to play the PGA Tour
        and give pro golf a try.

Q School is the shortened term for the PGA Tour Qualifying Tournament, a grueling six-day competition among men hoping to become golf superstars. More than 160 players compete over 108 holes, but only the top 30 finishers earn their PGA card, meaning they can play in Professional Golf Association events against the top golfers in the world. The PGA holds more than 40 tournaments each year, and the top players earn worldwide fame and millions of dollars. That's a lot of pressure at school!

The next 50 finishers at Q School are allowed to compete on the Nationwide Tour. Many successful PGA golfers started their careers on that tour. There are also several successful professional golf tours outside the United States, including the European tour, the South African tour, and the Japanese tour.

Q is also for the Queen of Scots, Mary Stuart, who became the first known woman golfer while living in France and Scotland in the 1500s.

A ball hit too far right or left will land in an area of tall, thick grass called the rough. Getting the ball out of the rough is always a tricky task. You can learn to hit the ball straight down the fairway if you practice hard enough. Another R, the driving range, is the place to do that. Golfers of all ages may grab a bucket of balls and practice their swings by hitting toward distant flagsticks.

R is also for the Ryder Cup, a competition in which top-ranked U.S. male professionals take on their European peers every two years. The Presidents Cup pits U.S. golfers against players from the rest of the world (excluding Europe). The Walker Cup, the amateur version of the Ryder Cup, is named after George Herbert Walker, the great-grandfather of President George W. Bush. Amateur women play for the Curtis Cup, and female pros compete for the Solheim Cup. All of these competitions are match play tournaments.

R r

R is for a grassy place
that makes the game so tough.
The tee shot missed the fairway.
It landed in the rough.

S is for a sand trap,
an easy place to reach.
But getting out is difficult.
You're swinging from the beach.

Sand traps, or bunkers, are large sand-filled depressions in the ground. From there, golfers use a special club called a sand wedge to loft the ball onto the green.

Swing also begins with **S**. Serious golfers are always trying to perfect their golf swing. Some basic tips for a good swing are these: Aim for a specific target. Keep your head still. Swing hard but in control. One of the smoothest swings belonged to another S—Sam Snead, who won a record 81 PGA tournaments in his career.

S is also for slice, which is a shot that curves sharply away from the golfer (to the right for a right-handed player). It is a common ball flight for a beginner. A hook is a shot that curves strongly the other way. A draw curves the same way as a hook, but in a controlled manner. A fade curves gently the opposite way. Talented golfers often purposely hit draws or fades.

From tee to green, Tiger Woods makes the loudest roar. He may be the most talented ever on the tour.

It seems as if Eldrick "Tiger" Woods was born to be the greatest golfer in the world. When he was only three years old, he shot a score of 48 for nine holes. When he was six, he recorded his first hole in one. Between the ages of 15 and 20, he won three U.S. Junior Amateur titles and three U.S. Amateur championships. Then he triumphed in three of his first nine professional tournaments. Three months later at the 1997 Masters championship, he recorded the lowest score in tournament history and won by 12 strokes—even though he was just 21 years old.

Woods finished on top in 40 of his first 149 PGA Tour events, including eight major championships. When he won the 2001 Masters Tournament, he became the first golfer to hold all four major professional titles at the same time (the Masters, U.S. Open, British Open, and PGA Championship). The feat became known as the Tiger Slam.

T t

U u

The U.S. Open has been played since 1895.

U is for the underdogs who often come alive.

Since 1895 the United States Golf Association (USGA) has organized the U.S. Open, which is considered the American national championship. The winner of that first 11-man tournament received $150. Today hundreds of professional and amateur golfers try to qualify for the U.S. Open, and the winner receives more than $1 million. No amateur has won the U.S. Open title since 1933, but the USGA, which serves as the governing organization for golf in America, also runs the U.S. Amateur championship and the U.S. Junior Amateur championship (for players under age 18).

Perhaps the most exciting moment in U.S. Open history was an unexpected victory by the ultimate underdog, Francis Ouimet. In 1913 the 20-year-old American amateur stunned the golf world by beating two famous English stars, Harry Vardon and Ted Ray, in a playoff. Ouimet's caddie during the tournament was just 10 years old! The surprise victory greatly increased golf's popularity in America.

V

V is for the Vardon
and the Vare, two trophies for
the professional golfers with
the lowest average score.

Between 1896 and 1914 British golfer Harry Vardon won six British Open championships and one U.S. Open title. American Glenna Collett Vare took six U.S. Women's Amateur championships in the 1920s and 1930s. Today their names are attached to trophies awarded to the players with the season's best scoring average on the PGA and LPGA tours. From 1999 through 2003 Tiger Woods became the first golfer to win five straight Vardon trophies. Kathy Whitworth won seven Vare trophies and a record 88 tournaments in her LPGA career.

The lowest single-round (18 holes) score in PGA Tour history is 59, which was first achieved by Al Geiberger in 1977. He finished 13 under par, an accomplishment so impressive that he became known as "Mr. 59." Since then, two PGA players have matched the feat in official events—Chip Beck in 1991 and David Duval in 1999. In 2001 LPGA star Annika Sorenstam became the first female professional to record a 59.

Hazards are obstacles that make play more difficult. If the ball lands in a water hazard, the golfer must add an extra penalty stroke to the score and take a drop, which is when the golf ball is dropped from shoulder height onto the course so that it may be played. The drop must occur at the point of the previous shot or at a point behind the water hazard.

W is the first letter in the World Golf Hall of Fame, located in St. Augustine, Florida, where exhibits are laid out like a golf course in 18 separate areas. The "Front Nine" is a journey through golf history, and the "Back Nine" focuses on the modern game. In between, a great hall honors male and female Hall of Fame members.

W is also for wondrous Michelle Wie walloping 300-yard drives. As a 14-year-old in 2003, she became the youngest-ever winner of the USGA Women's Public Links Championships.

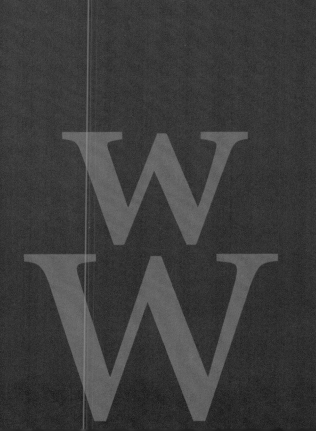

W is a water hazard—
a creek, a pond, a lake.
Hitting your golf ball there
can be a big mistake.

X marks the spot
     where the ball lands on the green.
Just fix the little ball mark
     and keep the course pristine.

"Etiquette" means practicing correct and polite behavior. It is an important part of golf, which is a game that values sportsmanship and fair play and requires concentration and a clean playing surface. Fixing the dent your ball made when landing on the green is only one form of golf etiquette. Other rules include the following: Replace any divots you make and rake sand traps to smooth out any footprints. Never bring golf bags or carts onto the putting green. Don't move or talk when another player is hitting the ball. The player whose ball is farthest from the hole always plays first. Never hit a shot when the players in the group in front of you are still in range. If the group behind you is playing faster than your group, stand aside and let them play through. And if someone hits the ball well, say, "Nice shot!" Hopefully, they will have the opportunity to say it to you, too.

Y is for the "yips,"
 when putting feels all wrong.
That's when a little four-foot putt
 can seem four miles long.

Y y

"Yips" is a term often used by golfers to describe the difficulties they may have in sinking short putts. Putting requires a very smooth stroke and a gentle touch, but many golfers find their hands twitching or jerking just as they're hitting the ball. Part of it is a reaction to the pressure of the moment. Golf can be a nerve-wracking game. Researchers at the famous Mayo Clinic College of Medicine have found that as many as half of all serious golfers have experienced the yips.

Even the best golfers in the world get the yips sometimes. There is a long list of golfers whose championships slipped away because of missed short putts. One of the most famous examples is Scott Hoch at the 1989 Masters Tournament. He just needed to sink an 18-inch putt to win the title, but he missed the putt! He lost the tournament in a playoff.

Mildred "Babe" Didrikson Zaharias was already a world-famous athlete when she started playing golf. At the 1932 Summer Olympics she set three track and field world records, winning two gold medals and a silver medal. She took golf lessons in 1933 and won the Texas Women's Amateur Championship two years later. Over the next 20 years she won more than 80 golf tournaments, becoming a founder and the biggest star of the Ladies Professional Golf Association (LGPA). Babe took her third U.S. Open championship in 1954, even after having surgery for colon cancer. She won by 12 strokes!

In 2003 several female golfers competed in men's professional tournaments, led by LPGA star Annika Sorenstam, who competed in the PGA Tour's Colonial Tournament in May. Five months later Se Ri Pak finished in 10th place in a Korean tour event. She was the first woman to advance to the third round in a men's pro tournament since... Babe Zaharias in 1945.

Babe Didrikson Zaharias. That's **Z**, our final letter.
On the track and at the tee,
was any athlete better?

Brad Herzog

Brad Herzog lives on California's Monterey Peninsula, just minutes from the Pebble Beach Golf Links. He was a guest columnist for the *Monterey County Herald* during the 2000 U.S. Open championship and has written magazine articles about everything from golf course architecture to his participation in the Masters of Miniature Golf, where he finished 31st out of 31 competitors.

Brad's previous books for Sleeping Bear Press include *K is for Kick: A Soccer Alphabet*, *H is for Home Run: A Baseball Alphabet*, and *T is for Touchdown: A Football Alphabet*. A past Grand Gold Medal Award winner from the Council for Advancement and Support of Education, Brad is also the author of *The Sports 100*, which ranks the 100 most important people in U.S. sports history (including a half-dozen golf pioneers). He has also written two American travel memoirs, *States of Mind* and *Small World*.

Bruce Langton

Illustrating children's books has been a wonderful experience and is a dream come true for Bruce. After a successful career in both commercial illustration and wildlife art, Bruce has switched priorities to focus on children's books and is now proud to add yet another to his list of accomplishments.

In addition to *P is for Putt: A Golf Alphabet*, Bruce has illustrated eight other children's books for Sleeping Bear Press including *Win One for the Gipper, America's Football Hero*; *B is for Buckeye: An Ohio Alphabet*; *V is for Volunteer: A Tennessee Alphabet*; and *H is for Hoosier: An Indiana Alphabet*. A lasting career as a nationally renowned children's book illustrator is Bruce's final goal in life. Today Bruce resides in Indiana with his wife Rebecca and two sons, Brett and Rory.